Perspiration,

Acorns,

Turnips

Also by Kevin M Sheetz

- Furniture

- Phantom Limbz

- To Seek Without Finding

Perspiration,

Acorns, Turnips

poetry and prose
by

Kevin M Sheetz

Perspiration, Acorns, Turnips
© Kevin M Sheetz 2020

Published using CreateSpace, LLC

ISBN-13: 978-1658684309

May all beings be happy,
may all beings be free from suffering.

CONTENTS

There the bodies are young, beautiful, whole; they flee toward one another with all certainty. The simulacrum still presents itself in its sparkling freshness, without resorting to the enigma of signs. There, phantasms are the welcome of appearance in the light of origin. But this origin is one that by its own movement recedes into an inaccessible remoteness.

- Michel Foucault, *The Prose of Actaeon*

But then it cannot well be said that this man has heard the Low Voice beneath the din of life or that he has gathered the Mystic Root in the field of the Void.

- Seng-chao

Sorry

I am become suddenly awakened in my bed, like a pear rising through the soot, the scaffolding of my dreams toppling into the vague darkness which greets my smarting eyes as they recollect their function of vision. Where am I? Who is this? Wherefore am I returned to being, to awareness, to the memory of all that has come before? I am no longer asleep. From beneath the blanket which enshrouds me, I produce my hands, pale shadows that dance like drunken birds and finally roost upon my face, my breath escaping them as from the bars of a prison cell. Sound slowly regains meaning, infiltrating my ear canals, my brain, my understanding, like water in its course. There is a gradual influx of sensation as I am once again myself. But I had never left. I am chained to this 'I' so inextricably that there would seem to be no separation. The thoughts gallivanting in my imagining are made clear in the same manner as the shapes surrounding me in reality. A coin spinning in the air like a mirror. A dolphin mid-leap infinitely vivisected by the phantom of time, a layer of dust on every action, a sponge absorbing itself, moist, foreboding. I get out of bed, my feet touch upon the floor, legs supporting the frame, trunk gently swaying, cranium swirling like a single particle in the vast array that culminates in planets, galaxies, universes, existence. A heart that beats like a sun, unheard, unfelt, unknown. Like no sun.

The sheets on my bed are cast aside. In darkness no shadows are distinguished. Before me is a sort of filter or veil; the further that sleep departs from me the more I can recognize it as being myself. Then what is it that dissipates? A cat delving into the shelf. Something scrambling for connection...

As Fashion Dictates / Foment

when life
seems
what does that mean?
what meaning is there
in seeming?
how does it seem?
in what capacity?
from which angle
that jarring shape
consumes our vision
the fragile inkling
that perhaps it might not be
all that it seems
but where does that idea
originate?
life does not seem
yet it is
it is only this
seeming
to be
with us
scratching and clawing and screaming
at the mirror
as if it were a disguise
we've grown sick
of wearing
a decoy

a pillar
in the desert
of the mind
vacant
bearing no weight
casting a shadow
into the wind
like a seahorse
becoming ensconced
repeatedly
disheveled
diffuse
parting ways
forever
time like a noose
forgetting to lay its eggs
on the back of an animal
asleep on the ground
breathing in
fractured and
broken
like an identity
unassumed
lowering the catafalque
against what seems
to be
insert
daffodil troglodyte
regained
in the ice
of life
melting always

in the forthcoming spring
galloping
hovering above the horizon
like an eel
tickling its basket
appearing it seems
tightly constructed
without flaw
fitted perfectly together
down to the lowliest molecule
grinning
awaiting the gaze of a microscope
to be discovered
even though it really wouldn't
change anything
an atom like a mother spider
with thousands of babies clinging to
its back
quietly trying
not to eat them
a human being
operating an automobile
strikes another human
simply walking
now splayed
in the middle of the street
a forest of heads
tongues going in and out
silently
cone eyes
beak nose
coral hair

opal mouths
opaque
dead human
in the road
oozing it seems
lackadaisical appearance
vying to outlive its donor
causal acquaintance
apprenticeship
the master is etched on a storm
tubercular
reality is spiny and evasive
spitting out something in its nest
a hive of living jewels
displaying the splendor
of the sun
a horse in the air
looking down on the shiftless clouds
anus of the heavens
downcast
unraveling threads
tied
to the hitching-post
of nothing
it seems
there is no great appraiser
no celestial stenographer
no divine clerk
balancing the ledger
there is not one side or the other
today is yesterday's tail
and the future

merely footprints
echoing into the distance
hazy
unremembered
sundown light
dark node
attached to wisps
shimmers in the air
a mirage
defecating by itself
a prism of smoke
exasperated
infinitely
dismayed
delayed being
clueless
tune
it's instrumental
this garbled understanding
born out of words
peculiar experience
not shared
exploited
minute by minute
continuous mass
ceaselessly gaining
explaining
what it seems
to me
a bird
has flown out of everything

untitled #1

there is starting
something like a new life
the hazy vision of mountains in the
distance
like the quiet murmuring of a stream
as it unfolds
in a wood
sunlight playing through the trees
I turn the corner
and consider which direction my steps
should take
what should I bring along
and what should I leave behind?
do I even have a choice in the matter?
the experience of these changes
could be like a violent wrenching
or a subtle shift
revealing again to me
what has always been there
waiting for my eyes
to chance upon them
as they once have before

Enclosure

the meadow
is painted on my mind
by a music
that comes from nowhere
the careful grains of sand
absorb the itching reeds
dilating spasmodically
like a flower
torn from the sun
a blue insect
collecting all the troubles
which sprout
from the eye
out of time
upon the ground
a shadow cast
by a ghost
trembling
like a goat
in spring
no iron bars
no broken legs
no fleeting glances
no fire
having to urinate
like a soldier
naked and

Bodhi

there are faces everywhere
whether I look at them
or not
a coat
hanging
from a nail
let peace prevail!
the twitching
shadows
of a mind
are obscured
a true feeling
wouldn't you like to know?
frankly it is astonishing
what the mind
concocts

Bronchial Forest

the waving nodules
swirl around
like confusion
an upset stomach
the burden of stones
tumbling through
crystallized abyss
gaping trapdoor
an imagination
fermented
by a rotted infinity
there is no production
nothing produced
no storage
the cilia like grass
an eternity
at every point of contact
golden touch
sharpness
stay the course
do not stay the course
coarseness
plasmate dispelled

Cool

walking this way and that
along a straight line
walking in this way
down the path of a dark mountain
a stream
sparkling with birds
the horizon traced
by the sound of the sky
the scattered trees
like objects in a dream
dust
freed from the earth
singing heavenward
like a bell
an ancient wall
crumbling
into time
with both hands

Not A Trace

the flight of leaves
from eyes
in the distance
a day in spring
dressed in arabesques
of sun and air
cool and clean
the unknown
gleaming

Flour on the Balcony

that which receives sensory
input
can be accentuated
with a ribbon
the teeth of a brush
pulled out
like a horse
a soldier tucked away
in a loaf of bread
soldering iron
the accumulating self
along the tire swing
shone blue dirt
history is the
record
of every bowel movement

it is not set in stone
that which suffers
that which does not suffer
it is

Muddy

dragonflies are sewn
under intricate
conditions
whether each web
must endure
the weather
a polarity
is sprung
against the grain
and hail
and earlobes
praying
like unfastened
rungs
abroad the patter
detailed
bygone heralds
a chance for the summit
crafting
all the while
pirouettes
graciously
demur
the sky
crumples
before long

struggling to think
with my head
instead
of my sphincter
which gasps
like a fish

In Parting

that which I seek to find
is not so far away
it's just o'er yonder
past my undoing
a friend in the heap
a climate to suit one and all
a man without fear
who feels no chill
a winter whose grandeur
is full of flowers
where forgotten words gain new
meaning
and the strain of what is lost
becomes weightless
I rub my hands over my face
as I look out across the sky
and dream again
of what it is
that could have been
but never was

Alien

one more teardrop that falls
even in this passing
moment
which will never come again
the same as me
a flickering flame
soon to be extinguished
by the whim
of a careless wind
much to my chagrin
the ceaseless whimsy of these gods
or fates
or whatever there is
that traces my steps
that shadows my thinking
the ones who look over
my every doing
I make a mess
all the time
seeking privacy
never to be found

A Star Made Out Of Sand

the curtains elapsed
transparent sparrow
gratuitous forthcoming
the astral palate
is singed blue rhizome
eggplants together
a coral sunset
is bleeding
apples
where are released
open salamanders
corralled into flames
of petrified
glands
globular nettles
spread eagle
outside bananas
a coughing fit
transgressing
cold folds
and tinctures
rhinoceros
priceless candle
training exercise
the pressure is
columnar
exposition

Genesis

The heaven and the earth
said in the beginning
there was a tree
of waters
and light was its fruit
God was a darkness
and it was good.
The firmament
was the sky full of cattle
the beasts were
formless men
and the third and fourth day
were as the first and fifth day
and it was good
inside the earth
which were divided
as God being naked
neither gold nor silver
fowl that tear the air
with their
foliage.
The multiplying dominion
of the seas
wherein a man and woman
are but dust and rocks
surging forth
a carrot.

for Thomas Bernhard

I am continually dispirited
as I stand before myself
the world forever following me
like a shadow
climbing over
all my footsteps
seeking that distant infinite
something or
other
those men and women
birds without a sprig
caught a network
serenade
suggesting perhaps a melancholia
shaped like a dynastic form
situated behind
the thinking
apparatus
which could use some oil
in order to call out
for this pecking
the man typing on a computer
silver, sleek
barren, ovoid
calamitous, disintegration
a self drifting yonder
like a song

a smog
the pollution of intention
befouling that which all eyes rest
upon
in passing
LOVE
what is it?
I've heard speak
I've seen wind
an umbrella coils the river around
blue ribbon
thunder
you know
it couldn't
it could be
it isn't
itching feast the feather blinks an orb
it is of stone
it is of the mind
tossed upon a leaf
a twig or branch
that is the baptism
the communion
of one to one to another once before
myself
standing and reading a disparate
shadowing
believe in you
believing in numerics
polysignificance
ribald
vulgarity

plaster kitten
marsupial banner
across the eternal nose
sneeze
into my heart
into my mother
into my municipal value
blue valve
callous
the sun glow
tickling a wave
cresting
like the decision to kill
oneself
made alone
without thought
within the window
upon whose sill
a dove alights
in an owl
alighting bolt speed
past the marker
the signpost
the ribcage of life cracked apart
to delve within
trying so diffidently
to live
by the tongue
of a sporadic divinity
carelessly kissing
a nearness
definition of sexuality

driven rain
bowing and retreating
too much
two too much
eagles distracted
by effulgent beauty
of the letters
you are reading
hopefully
hippopotamus
committing suicide
happily
the family
split anon
nowadays

skidoo
echoing

echoing

om

om
om
winter is

sighing

om

sapphire

Artifice

b and v
are identical squirrels
coming out of your mouth
jungles trailing open orifice
even the moon is different

Idiot

I've made a mistake
a tasteless decision
a tear in the fabric
of kindness
of hospitality
reeking like an exposed
brain
displaying the multiform
flag
of disparity
patriotism
plagiarism
despoiled
the lady in waiting
wailing
bridegroom
despot
intricately employed
despite all to the contrary
balcony from which
to hang oneself
as if expecting some solution
a ploy
anointed trickery
painful slab
of self-identifying slop

Do You?

bodies tend
to be in motion
obfuscated
by time
portending
their predilections
like leprous
scarecrows
startled
by their vacant
reflections
but oh
what fun
it is
isn't it?

Life Story

a growth of wild orchids
a heap of excrement
mountain lion seen through a shattered window
the sun hidden behind tall buildings
dust carried by the wind
petals floating on a river
the shadows of people on a bridge
an empty boat
a bed made and unmade
garbage tossed aside
the end of a brief rain
hands curled into fists
trains riding in the distance
landscape of sand
landscape of sound
birth and ruin
a sumptuous feast
full stomach
bleeding ears
a glass tipped over on the table

Player

a shape
descends
like a rainbow
in nobody's
imagining
and withers
without delay
like everything
else
witnessed
or unobserved
makes no difference
make of it
what you will
I'd rather not
naught
together

A Book

As I climbed the steps, a thought occurred to me. Were these steps infinite, and I tumbled, I would perhaps tumble down them without end, striking each identical surface with a different part of my body, feeling the pain of each instance of contact. This would continue indefinitely until I wasted away, first losing my skin, then muscle, then bone, etc. Until I was only a rolling head, with eyes bulging, tongue extended, hair coming out in clumps and strands, strands like saliva stringing along. The loss of my ears.

Jasmine Song

attachment to favorable
circumstances
and aversion
to difficult experiences
are the basis
of all suffering
to be unmoved
by the spasmodic fluctuations
of one's own mind
is true serenity
and peace
this song is easy to sing
but hard to embody
clear and bright
the transparent emptiness
of all existence
reality is a flagstone
corona of nothingness
full of bliss
throughout all space
and time

Abalone

when shall I be released?
will the circle be unbroken?
when where how why?
is it even possible
to leap these bounds
and cross
unmolested
into a purer future
one where tears do not fall
where light shines from every eye
I can only hope
to disappear
and leave not
a trace

Untitled #2

in the steam of longitudinal
harpsichords
dances a shiver
like a mayfly
discarded an inorganic partial
membrane
into the basket clasped to the breast
a forest shrinking into the eye
dangling obstructively
to regard this service
fortuitous or not
a distant blanket
enshrouded praline
sweetness that lasts
outliving the garbled memory
of lingering flames
at the bedside
in the courtroom
at the stable outline
of a thousand marching fish
perched on the table
a broken tablet
covered with sputum
in the autumn
at dawn
without waking

Untitled #3

imprisoned
like miners
in a crystal ball
balanced on the tongue of a moose
its head raised skyward
its fur heavy and rippling
four legs tail bones cigar
the cascade is loosened
according to the diurnal flagellations
a copse
in its own right
daring to precede
shark daffodil
layers flitting away
ever and ever
uncovering the morsel
the ground behind the atoms
four hundred legs
to stand upon
a diamond
mouse
rolling like dice
caught up
in fortune
and displayed stairwells
crimson

colic
festooned
by pleasure
dictation
the men are jettisoned quickly
a soul
in need of assistance
from distracted planets
circling the absence of light
like an ice rink
formed out from time
taken after
the fact
rinses its feet
dirt accentuates the contours of its
glop
sparking an indignation
of wiggling feelers
test each other
a confirmed silhouette
a situation
without border
without destiny
a skeleton is modest
perfume

Getting Up Early

my blue teardrops
my recollection of the swollen camel
the issuance from an edifice
withdrawn with the tightness
of olives
dancing into view
that oscillate stolidly
a carnival flagrant like a candle
loosened requisite
a diameter of guano
transforms the pallid frost
like a bluebird
cut open on the night
it's flattering
the novices
no longer recognize
the earth in a puddle
of water
with swift ears
eloping like snakes
in the drawer full of underwear
smells like a rainbow

Platonic Ducks In A Row

fruition
coming to completion
crossing the finish line
reaching the end
of the road
done with the book
returning to the source
origin
happily ever after
let's begin
becoming
the mouth that is a wellspring
fountainhead
carbonated thought
glorious summit highest peak
infinite threshold
boundless breast
the window open
vast eye permeating everything
marble being
the emerald a priori
golden
luminescence
dust of worlds
primordial consumption

the object
of all seeking
answer solvent
soluble divinity
practical water
sun and moon outside
moon and sun inside
weaver of souls
ceaseless activity
boys and girls
nectar of pullulation
liberal interpretation
liberation
fig tree growing
from the soil of forever

Christ Is Empty

an animal has left behind
tracks and crooked branches
to signify
its passing
a human being creates
a chair
for but one purpose
as if all things
were divorced
from one another
and there was no connection
an end in itself
which is no end
how painful
the origin of sorrow
to anthropomorphize existence
to impose purpose and meaning
where there is none
humanity a shapeless mass
a formless flailing around
within no boundary
an egg broke open
on the day

Active Solutions

winnowing through the
drainpipe of clouds
an emerald finger
beckoning
to the creation
of a further
entropic
barbiturate cranium
forsooth
a shard of butter
for the caravan to
pierce the
moonlight
which salivates
like a thirsty
god lusting
ornamented
by swollen
figments
particles
detritus ad infinitum
ex nihilo
birds swimming in reverse

The Everlasting Title

the body envelopes
comet teeth
a moon crying out its antlers
down they cascade
like vitamins
tools for the recollection
of a structure
housing a season
glimpsed in the meadow
a knife
a shadow
a desert laughing like rain
bowing toward the exit
anterior memory
anterior muscle
dexterity abounds
a coarse throat
passageway
to the embers
sunshine forbidden
living is accompanied
by stymied passion
billowing like countless bubbles
that pass into one another
the trees walk
on top of themselves

silver dancing
an announcement should be made
every living day
grieving for the tides
to be gone
across the final frontier
the race betrayed
with a step
forward
aplomb
dynasties
shatter like chandeliers
against time
the fullness of desire
and egregious fulfillment
together
in stone
enshrouded
body and life
the ceaseless living
it is noon
anon

Untitled #4

out of the cobra
my tousled hair
my scarlet
ambrosia
mouths full of soot
and pretty things
something sweet
lump sum
tender
drying
on the balcony
a nose too long
a bird
raining all out
gift of birthright
spoiled
baby legs

The Extent of the Periscope

A pony in a stable is guarded by the wind. The wind asks: "Another shelf?" The pony is oblivious, its head is stuck in a globe, it observes the outlines of countries all around its scope of vision. Tentatively, the little pony whinnied. Volcanoes burst across the world, earthquakes rattled the landmasses, mountains expelled avalanches like flatulence. The sky turned around and reflected a distant happiness. It flashed briefly across the wind and around the pony. Visibly upset, the pony licked and licked the entombing globe. Consequently, love spread like wild geese all over the place. Men, women, bright blue beetles, eggs, turnips, swallows, catsup, all began to shed love onto the ground. The globe developed a conical shape and two webbed feet drooped down from its point. Slowly, a grasshopper escaped the poor little pony's tear duct; when it spread its wings the colors sang a precious memory. The wind took hold of the shifting object which clung to the pony's head and whistled into it, at first very faintly, then quite loudly. Excruciatingly loud; the pony's ears wilted and formed a tribunal at the edge of the enclosure. The grasshopper held a very small willow tree which it guarded closely, with the stamina of a bull flying through the air. And the globe, due to the combined effort of all implicated, jettisoned off the pony's skull and landed on a train passing in the distance. It was never to be seen again, it donned a top hat and clasped a briefcase and rode the train forever into all eternity. That much is ascertained.

The stable was composed of nettles and thorns. They remained perfectly still, even with the carousing wind and the newly released pony. Then followed a silence, dripping and sputtering. Dimly, a crying was heard. The pony threw up. The wind went away. The grasshopper was of course very dainty, it struck a shell with a golden millipede and a multifaceted noise spilled out. A signal floundered along, parallel with the horizon, from which there were jutting tremendous antlers. They writhed like balconies and exuded a fragrance directly into the pony's forehead. Thereupon a cauliflower immediately grew and turned inside out, it leaked a gratuitous paste. The grasshopper became embedded in the paste. The miniature willow tree which it bore reverted to a castle, with devastating spires thousands of feet high. They clashed with the clouds which were solid as iron. They spoiled the mood by humming deeply with an elastic hymn. The paste clenched its ear as the grasshopper drifted into the air. Below it as it hovered, the ground was covered in steering wheels; the cars shone brightly with a lackadaisical malaise. From its vantage point the wind scoffed mightily. Its brow was furrowed like a snowflake exposing its genitalia.

The desert was propped up on its elbows. Wings were given freely. A lion rode by on horseback, gesticulating loudly. It apprehended the glittering erstwhile pony and presented it with a delicately crafted washing machine. The pony was at a loss for words. The lion vanished like a peacock. The antlers of the horizon beckoned.

Nobody was to be found. A reindeer was displayed rectangularly, possibly an omen of foreboding. Or perhaps foreclosure. The grass could soothsay but it wasn't allotted. A fever was born dancing. Its clicking shingles were of utmost posterity. The traps all enclosed. And now an invisible, inaudible fanfare, of soiled roses, loud as a demonstration.

Nesting in a tree of reality were several anteaters, their shadows were pangolins, dubious elderberry.

Not Alone

what you see before you
is Tao
the sounds entering your ear
are Tao
that aroma
is Tao
what you are feeling
at every moment
is nothing but Tao
we take part
in thinking
our life
is relationship
with Tao
the only thing
the fleeting joy
the lasting sorrow
when you wake up
in the morning
say hello

Computer Training

the tongue is loving
while an elephant
pries open
the cathedral
releasing thousands of
mosquitos
into the air
like sand
obscene bird
naked mirror
collapsing structure
ambling across the
open sources
qualified
for magnification
dire nutrition
the balloon is a microbe
sour
discreet

Noisome

the water
has growing amber
hair
that obscures
the passing emerald
with a sigh
a coiled scream
under length
takes a time
to become accustomed
weather
a dream
feet

Lying There

sometimes a feeling
shines through me
penetrating the
emptiness
of the mind
where God lives
not like a fog or cloud
dulling and
obscuring
but instead is like space
after rain
bright clear fresh
renewed
eternally
glowing with the
suchness
of being
where thought and action
disappear

Untitled #5

a fish is displayed in patches
eiderdown like a forked sorrow
twisting spire underfoot
centipede stems
a growth of brain matter
a horse pulled by a rope
toward a flagrant demise
bespectacled
the pillar is surprised
a basket of wrens
explodes
like a barn
the beaks can attest
when freedom begins
with salt
arrows
cashew eyes caught sidewinder able
bowl moon
ending with end
crying in the beginningless stage
a forest denuded
twice
by a rigid smile

Conjuration

slowly winding down the stream
accompanied by tall trees
which bend near the water
without touching
the jungle escalates immediately
once man's limits are left behind
trembling in the shadows
the heat of the blazing sun
penetrates every molecule
thoroughly
all the way through
the water creaks and groans
like an old house
the surface is green
blue
black
red in places
shifting
dissipating
coalescing
the trees deposit a leaf
their offering
their mute reverence
their ancient being
dancing beyond motive
contiguous

with mystery
where does this grow?
where does this take shape?
what is that
which endows all things with their
myriad characteristics?
to what end?
the birther of distinctions
a glowing lighthouse
a giraffe atop the grave of intention
sweeping the debris to make a nest
quiet
the rain is asleep
the eyelashes are downturned
fettered
hampered by lumps of luminescence
be quiet
the moon is listening
its sweat plummets
like a peacock
in the fold
a crossing of movement
isolated
by miraculous tendencies
nowhere betrayed
unimpeded
by the noose of observation
the nose of the mind
in all its glory
shoots out little pellets
of grief
confusion

misdeeds
splashed against the wall of reality
cement
misapprehension
panting heart eyes
a full moon blows its rattle
another thing is upset
the dawn is prickly
like a segregation
by firm hands
immobile moment
feebly tossing
breathing the glittering focus of the
present
before it turns away
ashamed
time is just looking
nowhere to be seen
collection of roots
shedding the dirt
like a beautiful little sun
in an aquarium
for the star eyes alone
they unfold
a toad barks
sacred chatter
frittering above
the mouth full of sand
winking like galaxies
a pair of underwear
with blotches and stains
the horse flows smoothly

past the siphon
of angels
clicking and ribald
jostling their holy private parts
the sound of crickets is produced
it is a heavenly order
a decree
parted with
at the meeting of two
flowering blood forms
searching for the right mote
the identical majesty
set apart from the herd
of magic
and bees and buzzards
entranced
unable to flit
sideways
through the long mist
of seashells
bleeding tiny seahorses
into full grown hair
speared by the diamond
night
galloping steadfast
belonging close by
a brief lapse
in the seasons
celestial bed-wetter
incestuous divinity
multiplying like mice
out around a grasping floating

breeze
loosening its earlobes
which are starting again
to trigger
the apoplexy
the apologetic demon
bathed in gourds and mummies
socks
pots and pans
plants elaborating the appeal of
numeration
the mind is putty
dough
bread rising in no oven
no overt attachment
pending
approval
the family expels together
a fungus rapidly into the sky
the written plea
for clementine rotation
bedridden
name
staking a claim
informant
the tissues are all used up
salami disappears rigidity blots the
bandaged
lagoon
wherein toils the lowly
race of legumes
marching along the turtle's spine

compiling uses for the air a horse torn
into ribbons of
rust
gutted bellows
the blasphemy of the toothbrush
engenders clitorises upon the sky
downfall
of damp slumping leaves
weeds
tricks pink igloos
sprouting foundational diseases
meant to find a host
a plethora of hosts
meant to inundate
the living scraps
of earth
that dig their tusks in the worms
that try to hide their tusks
their pincers
their explosive ballerina
lying flat on the table
of effluvium
emulating
immolating
the tired apparatus
touches down
slapping a forehead
blue with groundless mutterings
that do not spill forth
that cannot come out
undone
toes of the spaces between stars

planets
spatulas
eggplants pained and extinguished
like tarantulas
molding
other books trickling
beside the light
that mewls
bed pin
feature
underwater cordiality
make-believe behaviors
ready material spent
open atom
what can be expected to emerge?
to where this emigration
like a tide of rinds
disheveled from their fruit
the body
lidless beam
supplant ivory corn forgot
the letters traced icicles scream
a bicycle elapsed
snow unscrewing its trunk
from the base of all feelings aside
a bitter fly races despite the stream
grouped according to preference
a big steaming mistake
thudded on the ceiling of the earth
and carcasses fell out
standing one on top of the other
like jade plumage

like moisture
palanquins are pubescent
in the array of
unknown festivals
wreaking music atop the lambs
spangled death beep
protruding information
untoward
a silk realm
broken by sticky elation
caused
in the course of doing and not
by a price
the monetary value
is deception
there is a porpoise
over there
at the fence which needs a bell
and a cadaver to peel
the blowhole crunches
like a disturbance
there is none

Untitled #6

through the window
a fox lopes along
in the back yard
looking for food
looking around
a fox as the sun trails down
behind the horizon
of trees
wet from rain
a bird sings

the blueness of a star
is measured in relation
to its depth
the rear horn
of certain animals
is said to produce the vibrations
of a harp
struck gently

the flight of a stork
determines the radishes
from now onward

the sun is in the meadow
like a cow

A Friend

the breasts float like hair
as they inspect the grounds
a circumcision
a golden drop of water
which exfoliates
like a steering wheel
guiding the porcupines across distinct
trickles
an effulgent itching
careful bending of light
abdomen rippling like a sail
catching the sea's sneezes
and mitigating
a flock of migration
untold stories

To My Grandmother

not so long ago
I looked into your eyes
and saw there a sun
as it sets
and now the night
has gathered you
away
to where you and I
must someday go
I can only hope
that you may finally
lay down your weary head
to rest
on those heights
where angels weep
and gain their wings
I love you, Grandma, always

If You Were Me, Then I'd Be You

I may be just a man
falling down
trying to crawl
out of himself
and scrape together
some semblance of living
like a shred of cloth
lost in escape
from the enemy
that enemy who lives neither here
nor there
just inside
a voice trailing away
from your ear
what does it say?
I cannot make out the words
though I try to write

Untitled #7

this whole world as it spins
and tosses and turns
sometimes can be
very cold
and make you gasp
for breath
and it sometimes can be warm
and make your heart
teem with love
there are people who
mistake
one for the other
do you know
that they are the same
the good and the bad
the starlight that shines
upon the glade
the death and the life
a mother and her child
shivering
even in the heat
that comes
when an eye closes
and another opens
lashes fall
whether you like it or not

I'll Fly Away

and leave this tired world behind
I'll pick up these feet
and make my way
to a land where hearts do not break
and love is never ending
where I do not make my parents
unhappy
and no one worries for me
this world that populates my mind
I'd like to share it with you
I'll give it freely
if you please

Miss You

do you hear that sound?
the sound of nobody suffering
of footprints on a mind
free of violence
where plants and animals grow
where egos proliferate
yet do not cause harm
I aspire
to trickle down
like the rain
I reach out
mouth open
revealing vanity
someday

Brain

drinking champagne
in Oklahoma City
I noticed the sky
is quite large here
and the people
I happen to talk to
have a beating heart
just like mine
and hopes and dreams
and such
I imagine
that there are things
that bring tears
to their
eyes
and I feel
it too
I feel all the Ten Thousand
Things
the same as you
thank you for being
a friend
in this
interminable
mess

Yonder

expelling urine
from out my body
with enough force
to dislodge the freight train
between the legs
of an overlarge woman
straddling the embankment
clothed in mice
blanketed by mermaids
singing a tune
a folk song
a mélange
a menagerie
thrice reinforced
by glittering magnates
and obfuscated principles
lined up on the border
of escalating
comeuppance
thither

Daylight

when I got to work today
I left my keys in the car
later
passing a window
I happened to see two ducks
alight upon the surface of a lake
in the distance
I only saw it
for a second
in my passing
yet still it filled me
with something
great
that overflowed
my meager cup
something
that isn't there
even the water in the toilet bowl
sparkles with the clarity
of a diamond
when I woke up this morning
a song played in my head
'all the words and the wine,
make-believing they were mine'

Fragments of a Poem

why am I so deeply
unhappy?
what poison is this
that infects my brain
and makes me unable
to be
who I am?
wherefore do I strain and grope
in the darkness
searching for some shred
of meaning or purpose?
and still I dream
and still that noisome foulness
that lives inside my mind
urinates into the tottering
cup
that was fashioned
in the likeness
of my soul
I am alone
like a stone
like an idea
like a dream
forgotten upon waking
by the trill
of birds

and the sun's
golden rays
slanted upon the ground
and still I dream
and still the weightless motes
perhaps offer instruction
in the way
I should live
someday discovering
an illimitable
sacredness
as I delight
in my own
dissolution
and become adopted
entire
into a nameless cosmos
delving without care
into the fantasy of being
into the grotesque charade called life
into the phantasmal abysses of reality
in vain do I try to recall
the exact moment
when I went
astray
the precise unit of time
upon which I stumbled and fell
within the cavernous aperture
that in long eons past
was once a man
or perhaps merely an empty space
unbegotten

Stardust Memories

the reason
for the sunlight
is difficult to establish
what dust is there
upon the ground
and above
when the shining orb
has returned
to its nest
remnants persist
and show themselves
wavering
yet unmoving
the treasures
that are disclosed to us
skittering
and yammering
between the buildings we've erected
and the trees we haven't
are perhaps there to remind us
that the mind is a little thing
and the body feeble
the emotions
and thoughts
and feelings
that we imagine

to be the material
of our being
are really nothing but
pulses
of the breeze
as it turns over
each grain of sand
only to reveal
the truth:
vacuity

Avocado / Pomegranate

standing
like a chair
in shirt,
pants,
shoes perhaps
a being
carved out of the marble
of infinity
an opening mouth
a tear suspended
from an eye
like the crest
of a wave
crashing
on the shore
of nothing
a table
like a hen
laid
forgotten promises
like distances
long ago travelled
in the staircase of my memory
reclining
like a god
in the meadow
of my imagining

Mercy

when I hold it in my hands
it falls away
within the fathomless
chasm
of my heart
a bird is singing
it is the sound
of the world
and
I am cast
like an anchor
from the deck of a ship
lost at sea
and I resound
like the sunlight
as it hits the ground

It's a Process of Creation

the hummingbird contracted
into a single polar climate
trail etched
bright submarine slope
while yet passive
and collected
a stream
dangles from the heavens
isthmus of
paltry distribution
the dendrites reached
a fever pitch
and the
altitudes scattered
craven whispers

Brochure

a dugong
full of angels
and the kindness of strangers
helping a poor boy
with God in his eyes
and blood on his hands
this life sometimes is beautiful
and in the sun and sand
I am sometimes so filled
with love
that my eyes are bounded by
tears
thank you so much

the cool breeze
which originates
in the mind
blessed function
of the soul
in opposition
a canopy
displaying
the wealth of stars
scattered
like stones
in the river of my life

Fraternity

beyond the pall
of sense
there reigns
a silence
when I am
confused
I call it by a name
'Great One'

Untitled #8

a boat that does drift
upon a restless tide
making some worthless poem
when a boy
should be asleep
the grave calls
I heed it not
I am not afraid
I stand guard
against the tide
of the things that I should do without
yet hold tight to my breast
the reader of this forsaken nonsense
ought to regard it
with a grain of salt
and breathe easy
as someday I hope
to do
when the sun
smiles
and lays a weary body down

Short Peaces

you can call it instant happiness
instant good feeling
tumbling upside down into a
cavalcade
look me again in the eye
the one that doesn't blink
like a broken wristwatch
money flows freely given
bloody
running away

the last thing I remember
I was walking through myself
and I thought I heard me
call out my name

a bald spot on the soul
where hair
no longer grows

a blue sun rose over the grass

what I want
isn't on the menu

time does not move

these things are endlessly
complicated
the process of division
is infinite
there is no solid ground
no empty sky

God is a pervert
a sexual predator
the cosmic pedophile
manipulating
and taking advantage
of all creation
to satisfy Its whims
and divine urges
the celestial rapist
absolute incest
the continuous nightmare
of existence

movement is still(ness)

'is' resembles a block
of marble
which cannot be broken
'is not'
like smoke
cannot be grasped
both are chains
that bind

'I am' is relinquished

and yet still I yearn
for where there is no sea
and no cities
where I can flit
like a dolphin in my mind
where there is no space
through which to fall
echoing across the stagnant eons

when I have five fingers
a grain for each one

I swell with rain
where there is no dancing
system

the (wooden) club
is blubbering

the mind tends toward clinging
always searching for something to grasp

the traceless self
abides nowhere
the pathless mind
is freedom

the forest is a breeze
when it sparkles
like a grape

I had forgotten that I was suffering

one evening I stumbled upon
an elephant farm
in my broadest awakening
I drank from the muddy river
and coiled my eyes
into snail shells

the substance of the world
is like that of a reflection
on a window
glimpsed in passing
a momentary recognition
then nothing
scattered like leaves
by the wind
there is a tide
within my mind
that ebbs and flows
without a sound
the same as the planets
that swirl through
the galaxy
effortlessly
without care
or worry
the intricate workings
of this wondrous mystery
the crystalline stillness
of life

God lives outside mind
Self dwells beyond thought

Take Care

I've found
that I've laid a rutabaga
in all possible futures
a rope
that dissolves
within a panoramic
frequency
the nomenclature
discloses
heavily the forested
steps
on a quivering gale
tickled
bushel of crab apples
hectare

Summer Dead Weight

the effect of words
upon the brain
can be observed
through the flakes of moustache
that become noticeable along
the spinal pan
as it distorts
the surrogate hemisphere
a light trawling
apparently
distends as if
taken for granted
by the vast siphon
that gathers it

Remembering

it is true what people say
a dragonfly
as sweet as a cherry
can light a million candles
with the dew
of tears
shed upon a hunchbacked whale
dazzling
into the multitudinous
streams
of a swollen belly
a dying eye
before it is
a swarm

Therapy

opening out of a flower
was a summer day
the response of an eyelid
lashes twitching
like a thousand butterflies
cloistered
by the arms of a train
stumbling in the rain
a forest
grows hair
which drastically
escalates
forward
albeit a planet
the size of a balloon
whisks away into the light
to forgo
all identifying valuations

Land Ho!

a leaf is falling
the wind rises over the island
water all around
the globe
land of hope
hopeless land
the seed of dreams
priceless country
swallowed by the day
and night
galloping buffalo
spewing out its song
like sand
like dusk
like ears
go to her
she is calling
the light stretches out
brimming
sally forth
tally ho
ominous homeward
scratch

Breathing

there is a body
outside of this one
there is a mind
within the one
(that is) full of thoughts
which swarm like bees
that congeal
like a storm cloud
a mind and a body
let them fall away
become aware
of the expansiveness
that goes beyond everything
there is a limitlessness
where you and I
are no longer there
are no longer separate
where there is no separateness
where is and is not
before and after
dissolve into now
and the now
drifts away
like a petal
expanding, contracting
be patient

A Roadmap

a wheel spinning
in the reflection
of an eye
wild horses running
pineapple currants
across the earth
within the sky
above the universe
uncovering
the activity of the self
something in the bottom
of a well
what is it?
how does one gain access?
a handprint
in the sand
authentic familiarity
personal cosmos
osmosis
transcendent psychosis
a broken system
comes to fruition
with the finality
of space
gleaming
basic needs

tide of grain
sprouting
turmoil and harmony
unshielded
almond

is
are
and
a
the
like
an
with
to
from
as

fortress
clothes
terminal ice floe

It Takes So Long To Hang A Rose

a magistrate has killed the tramps
the shadows lie unannounced
the tropical dandy beautiful smell
the clockwork nostril is unsuspected
a is turbulent
b is connected
c disposes of transport vaccination
the heels spring ether
a light goes along in spades
the reason is not plied
a marigold suffers the little hoses
donkeys
heirlooms large and frothy
the magnate is murdered in the snout
a banana reveals its distance
gasping at the seams
tresses tickle and explain
all the horoscopes wink
a delicate capture
dismal wherewithal
the armed forces belong
kaleidoscopically
translucent feelings wither angels
a beard runs amok
a steward is missing
the plane hisses and breathes

the clothes are folding themselves
a will stiffens and extracts
the periodicals slash and bite
cruel tightness in the splinters
the rule is split aside
the coroner is pleased
a body dynamited infinitely
a braying distraction
colored hoops and whistles
panther contradiction

Untitled #9

Onan plucked at his feathers, his eyebrows were
heavy, they jutted out of his forehead like soup tureens.
He raised his hands to the sky, he lowered them to his
feet. The vault of heaven remained intact. Onan became
infuriated, the marble staircase leading away from him
glistened with ocular secretions. He took out his pipe and
place some material into it. He lit a match on his nose
and threw it away, the flame vanished thickly. A name
bred in concentric whiteness. Onan blackly reveled.

Outward Snow Forever

ceiling inflation clemency untoward
redundant
coupled squeezing tryst cyst
dramatic furlough collecting district
haven
heaving spiral elevation simply
frog noose collar balcony red
glamor seedling circus quell rib
trench bolt five
drips assert festering humid bulge
axiom velvet bundle
endeavor
years budding hamlet freshening
diode interruption health banal corner
sixteen weather sliver
basket hat
dangled inure ululation
scorn
fief food sever revere gumption
plastic return
irreality grandeur
pastoral tribulations egregious
moment
rarity blow wastrel
mussels
justly

Heart Mind

such is
the body of transformation
that the trunk
of an ibis
collapses
into a forest
shadow
on the ground
living eel
eyeball fish stuck out
transpired
eventual eclipse
to release
the instant sound
lion
of the rain across
distances
inescapable fork
and forming
almost together

Noses

a lion arrives on horseback
gesticulating loudly
through a prism
the future is seen
through a sphere the past
can be observed
through a pyramid the ostrich
of birth
the ostrich of the present
languishes on tides
of rice
a peculiar settling among
the branches and
pinafores
fallen in the river
the antelopes burn like pistons
through the open door
it's time for bed

Plate of Cranes

a ham
placed
in the elevator
brain cornea
itself
to blame
in the air
a plain
a plaint

Coat Rack

the ass of a cigarette
has dirt stuffed in the hole
it whinnies like a lobster
and becomes shrill as the night
sits down on its face
like a bowl of minnows
that secrete onions
so that nothing is identified
and a quarrel arises
between the bed and the
stave which takes a drink
from the stifled garters
of a hare
who has rubbed a pinch of saltpeter
on the window
without refrain

Lavender

the lilac birds have sprung to mind
facing east
and feeling nothing but time
in water and sand
the air ambulates in all directions
serpentine sensation
of what has come before
and around
and after the fallen wind
gradated gamboling
the winsome beings touch each one
a secret is firmly dislodged
it is the crown dripping with berries
atop perfumed mucus
miraculous armadillo
perfunctory jubilation

Dancing Outside The Medicine Wheel

("it's all center, and nothing is without")

the sky has no eyes
the earth has no hands
the wind has no mind
the spirit has no body
the being is weightless
the noise is soundless
trees grow
within the heart

AUM

Made in the USA
Monee, IL
10 June 2020

33072457R00066